Wrong T
Hom

War Poems

It makes you wonder who won.

BY THE SAME AUTHOR

Poetry available
Makers and Destroyers
Love's Troublesome Journey
The Belt Room
Scotland's Saint
The Sex Doctor
Curriculum for Excellence

Poetry coming soon
Surveying the Wreckage
Janet: A Life in Verse
Epiphany Under Azure: Columba on Iona
Likabehandlingsplan
Queens of the Reich

Biography coming soon
William Wallace (re-issue in Scots and English versions)
Robert the Bruce (re-issue in Scots and English versions)

Wrong Ticket Home

Glenn Telfer

Certain that someone out there likes this stuff.

Published By
Big Ride
6/3 Pinkhill Park
Edinburgh EH12 7FA
Scotland

A catalogue record for this book is available
from the British Library.

ISBN: 978-1-909297-12-8

Cover by Glenn Telfer

Design by Wordsense Ltd, Edinburgh

CONTENTS

The Commando Monument

PART 1

Audrey drove me here because this is where
they say you trained and I want to be
close to you in this special year,
when you've been gone for sixty of them,
sixty. Sixty waiting years. You'll know,
if you know anything, that I don't need

an anniversary to be reminded.

When you decided I thought you seemed
an unlikely commando; can you kill
with kindness? Even after you came back
from Scotland and I nearly swooned
with desire at what they had done to
your body when you took off your shirt;

our daughter that night.

As their reputation grew so did I with pride
you looking like a god, your old wardrobe
given to scrawny cousins and still so gentle
even though, as you must have been, its
opposite sometimes. Making Audrey stories
with you as the hero you really were

fighting crocodiles rescuing Goldilocks.

Fear a thing in my stomach always, but
I banished it as you must have done. And
have done since every single day since
that day. And although married again and

well to a decent man that surrendered me
time with you, gave our child siblings, but not

a single day have you slipped from my mind

like having two husbands and two parallel lives
both real in their allotted realms and crossing
over through Audrey. But here, now, just the one
in this godly place half way up a mountain
and almost journey's end. *Long way for a cup of tea,*
and I hear the smile so obvious in your voice.

And I say back, *Not when you're here too!*

PART 2

And sixty years coming here
a heart ache big as this sky
feels somehow lessened
by the magnificent scale

the clouds, silly thought really,
carrying all the tears away
to be renewed as rain somewhere
perhaps over France falling

as a blessing on your rectangle
as it falls on mine resting
against the plinth with my
little girl's words copied fresh

for this day to stake my now
ancient claim for the glory
plucked from the highest branch
that is your estate

and my inheritance and recompense
for your absence.
This piece of paper the balance
against a life forfeited, although

not just yours or mine, and
claiming the inner brightness
contained in the prayer starting,
Dear Daddy,..

The Great War

FIRST FRIGHT

...tightening the straps, cycle the bolt. Right! A
quick private prayer, said so many times now it's a
mantra; *Let me go back to my family and my wee
girl.* Officer fixated on his watch, then the whistle
and up the steps and over the line on that day
between the us and them, in both senses

that line crossed again rummaging
in the drawer I came across a photo
in a fancy gilt frame never before seen
to me, an unknown soldier, curious
I took it through, *Who's this, Granny?*

She stopped dead stunned silent
and I saw, for the first time ever,
a sudden terrible pain, perhaps even
a fear in her eyes and a glazing
that could not be held back

by her iron will.

The atmosphere in the room
charged with an electricity from
another world as that terrible day
returned after half a century and
he stepped back over the line when

his ghost just walked into the room
and flung his bonnet down and she
became a girl again. Seeing her fear

I got such a fright as I've never had
since. *It's ma big brother.*

He died in the war.
I miss him so much.
And she took me in her arms
comforted my panic and perhaps
unknowingly I comforted hers.

Another half century has passed
She, like he, is gone now and I'm
the only bearer by proxy of that
burden, a breaking one in weak
moments when I think of that

first fright

and the odd thoughts that spin off
from it; the cousins I never had,
the man I only knew through
her love and a photo, but
a burden can be a privilege too

when I think of the fierceness
of her love for him that runs
through me to carry until my day
to cross that line between the us
and the them

and claim the kinship with
that terrible glory
contained in the dead man's penny
and my granny's tears.

JAMES
KIA: 22/09/1918

It is the tiniest of details
on which to build a life:
He sometimes had a boiled egg
for his lunch, but
would forget to bring it in
(this was before he was married)

and mum would say, "Look,
he's left his lunch again!
Run along and hand it in."
I loved doing that because
he was my big brother
and I was his favourite.

Whatever plans he had
for a future in the soap works
clashed with the Kaiser's plans
for the future of Europe.
He didn't mind at all
a wee trip abroad with his gun.

He loved the army.

So joined the Territorials.
He used to bring his rifle home
and leave it in the corner.
"Don't touch it," as if the girls would.
He'd clean it on the table.
Mum said, "Get that thing away."

Champin' at the bit
he had to wait until May '15
until the 7th Bn made the trip.
Not the one-way single to France
of workmates and neighbours,
but a longer Med cruise for

a surprise picnic at Gallipoli.
Guess who got the surprise?
The Turkish reception served
Maxim and barbed wire for hors d'oeuvres,
before settling down to a main course
that was just as hard to swallow.

Turned out that Johnny Turk
knew how to use a machine-gun
as well as Fritz or Hans.
Then the shame and relief
of the retreat back to Egypt.
Christmas 15,16,17 came and went.

And James learned the hard way,
'clearing objectives with the bayonet...',
that the Holy Land was no sight-seeing
soft option for the biblically inclined.
The only holiness, they joked,
was in the arse of their breeks.

The obscene madness of those moments
in the trenches and bunkers;
"Effendi, Effendi!", as they were spitted.
The filth and flies, dysentery and malaria

almost neutralised by the official language
in reports, but not in the memory.

Any thoughts that James had
of missing out on the big show
were put right when they shipped
to France in April '18
to try their luck in the great
mincing machine that was

the Western Front.
He came through the Battle of Queant
in September 1918
and prepared for the next one
the real killer of a job:
Breach the Hindenberg Line.

Jerry was near finished, they said
running out of sauce maybe
but they still had plenty of the killing stuff
from the death bottle
to go around.
And then, a lucky break

a deserter to be escorted
home for Court Martial
James, the escorting sarjeant.
A minor miracle had left him
unscathed in all the years of killing
had he got the magic ticket out of it?

The Germans were near done.
And maybe it would be done

bar the dusting and the March
through the Brandenberg Gate
by the time the trial was finished.
He dared to hope

although it ran counter
to his nation's genius
that he might have fixed bayonet
for the last time,
victory parade excepted; Wait,
don't get ahead of yourself!

Webley holstered he made the trip
to Blighty. Following orders,
talk was functional only.
Arriving St Pancreas, a functional request.
Un-cuffing the prisoner
for the toilet cubicle

standing arms folded positioned
to prevent a sudden dash into the crowd,
as if he'd be so daft.
Come on you in there. Ur ye haein a bath?
And then, the thought, somewhat light-hearted,
I wonder if there's a back window?

The grue ran up his spine,
he pulled the pistol and kicked
in the door to find no bath, but clean escaped!
And disappeared into the trench system
of his own manor. Local boy,
did he know these lavvies

or was it just luck? But, ...
losing a prisoner for Court Martial,
only one outcome; Court Martial.
Oh, the irony, ending up
escorting himself for CM. Guilty!
Reduced to ranks, returned to regiment

in short order, ready for the final push to Berlin.

He was just one of many
that never made that trip
this side of oblivion.
They said it was a sniper's bullet
a precision to match
the crisp precision of the telegram:

It is my painful duty to inform you
that a report has been received from
the War Office notifying the death of :-

The same story repeated all over Europe
millions of times and
in an instant everything changed forever
something stops and goes a different way.
The wait for the telegram is over
a despondent road is the view ahead.

Mum's face transformed into an old person.
The bright glow that would surround him
when he turned the corner and came up the close
that sustaining thought that she
had held so fiercely in four years
of appalling headlines, dimmed

and something broke inside her.
I was only a wee girl
but I mind the air sucked out of the room
suddenly hearing the clock tick loudly
as seconds passed like years
people saying stupid things.

Dad just sat down and bent forward
with his face in his hands. Blank
and silent.
An invisible monster grabbed my heart
and squeezed it *I kept thinking,*
I'll never take him his egg again.

Our family died there too
as surely as if we'd all been shot.
The moment passes and life goes on
you forget but not really
every single time I have an egg
when I did my washing

and took up the carbolic
he came into my mind
and mum not the least bit scared
of death because it would bring her
son back to her arms.
Her big lovely son

wi his daft ideas of adventure
like all the others boys
up the close in every street in this land.
Hear him say, "Where's ma dinner, Mum?,"

one more time. Him smelling so clean,
Ye knew when he stepped up the close.

but now not and that forever
in this life.

In that tiny space of our lives so much grief
Ma big brother, jist one of them.
Oh, James! The pain still
seems like yesterday. And it will only go
when they close the lid of my coffin.
For the which, I'll thank God.

MY DASHING
HIGHLAND DARLING

Had you lived for me
this would have been our summer
four weeks of sunshine
a strange fate for Scotland.

Going long walks every day
or taking the train off the map
arms round shoulders or
just sitting holding fingers

you still in your kilt and saying,
But Man, dae I look braw!
They'll run when they see your knees,
I said. But they didn't.

This glorious weather brightens
the mind and sackcloth grey
with misery becomes
a precious golden shawl

brought here for this moment
the sun sweeping his bright arm
in amber over the field
where we would have our picnic;

ginger beer, cheese sandwiches,
a boiled egg for you to juggle with
and show off. And then, then
ma highland lover

we would lie on the blanket
and after we would laugh again
at the thought that you'd never
even been north of Springburn.

von Richthofen Triptych

1. THE RED BARON;
A FAMILY CONNECTION

Visiting grandparents, I took along my latest,
the red Fokker Triplane to show Danny
who immediately recognised it and established
the direct link between the baron and myself.

I saw them once, he said,
as he held the little toy up high at 1/72 scale
the ceiling becoming in his mind's eye
the Flanders sky 50 years earlier

you could easily see the red colour
from miles away. A dozen of the baron's boys
attacked in waves like sharks
a lonely observation plane which

twisted for a few pathetic seconds
when the Spandau's faint tapping
reached the trenches as the machine guns
stitched a line of bullets

for the airmen's shrouds
along the flight path until smoke
turned obscenely quickly to flame
and the thing spun gently as a broken butterfly

as if it could land lightly without hurting
the crew except it was on fire......
*My God, what a death, I couldn't look
and was hoping crew already killed,
give me a sniper or mortar bomb any day.*

*We heard a cheer from the Huns
carry across no man's land
in the cold air and Billy punched
the fire-step planking in anger
and hurt his hand.*

Handing the little toy back
he returned to 1965 and
remembering his orders
went into the kitchen to
sort out the tea.

Later, leaving, he secretly slipped me
a half crown to even things up,
*Here, ..get a Sopwith Camel.
We cannae huv the baron ay
having things his ain way.*

2. TROPHIES

From the Junkers bloodline came the inheritance
that made it all possible: the hardness,
the iron grip of duty, the need for mission
and the prowess in the hunt; the queen gene
that tied it all together as death

in over 80 victories.

All that 'knights of the air' stuff, you bought into it.
Imagining the machine as your destrier.
Having little trophy cups made of each success
in the joust as if ripping someone's head open
was a game to be remembered as winning.

Well, it felt like that at first!
When you had the energy and optimism
to counter-weight the deaths
you witnessed and caused with your
cursed skill in boar hunting,

a skill which transferred easily to Englanders.

April 1917, you really hit your form.
Dispatching 22 Britishers in a month
your look almost killing by itself as it
willed the angry ribbon of bullets
to the enemy pilot.

By then you had become the machine
you flew and fought in
crude simple, but clever in certain ways

connected with killing.
It was what you were destined to be.

But with destiny achieved, something happened
to the boyish and chivalrous ritter,

perhaps you just grew up
and your arena, the bonfire in the sky
with its flaming Englishmen leaping
from their cockpits, didn't seem
so sporting anymore.

The fan mail from tasty fräuleins (pics included)
epistles from graveyard ghouls
the patronage from the Kaiser's family
baying Caesars at prisoner slaughters
and you their favourite executioner

a golgotha with a Spandau.

And something dies, as it always does,
when life is seen clearly
the emptiness of everything you had become
the illusion of the heroic
your ugly journey

from light-hearted game to grim business
from boy with a future to a killing machine with trophies.
Your cups, the hellish reminders
of your gift and, you must have known,
your future as someone else's trophy.

Near the end you became chaotic
sleeping badly, by turns timid or reckless
nerves frayed beyond the power
of coffee or schnapps to still
nothing sorts the dread feeling

except willpower and then only briefly
when you summon the
ghost of your younger self,
the boyish young baron,
in the mess or for a visiting relative.

And so, as it must,
there comes the reckoning and
a part of you welcomes it as a trade-off,
the Devil's price worth paying, against
a future which would be a life with ghosts

burning screaming friends and enemies
indistinguishable in their torment.

After the countless thousands
of rounds fired at you
it is strange that your circus shut
with a single round as if the snap
of a jealous god's finger

as a marksman you would have admired
the economy of one bullet
and its perfect placement
the full stop on the page
of the last paragraph of your life.

3. THE HEALING PROCESS

Let's look at enemies, Boys and Girls.

Coming across an old educational magazine
in a box in the school's resource room
I note its date, April 1968,
and could remember it hanging fresh
from the newsagent's string
on the 50th anniversary

of the Red Baron's death
by fair play in a game of machine guns
over the Somme, which the magazine
commemorated in its Man of the Week feature
with British fair play still in evidence
as it noted with not a hint of irony:

*A scourge to the British, but a fine pilot and an honourable
and sporting adversary, as much admired by his enemies for
his iron nerve as his gentlemanly conduct.*

A view corroborated by his burial
with full military honours *by us*
who knew by cruel experience what sort
of hard opponent he was, but saw
their own frailties in his death and
saw the same human in him as in us.

That generation, more than any,
knew how fate evens thing
out over time on the killing floor
with the baron and his Hunnish ilk

as the unwitting catalyst
in the healing process

a strange but eventually effective balm
for the wounds that nations
inflict on each other
over a surfeit of pride or greed.
meanwhile on the new killing floor
seven blast-safe floors down

air conditioned in a comfy seat
flying your drone into combat
daily facing the risk of eye strain
or indigestion and the hypocrisy
of clearance at the highest levels
the opposite of the healing balm.

SE5a

delight and surprise were equally off my scale
as I saw it sitting all alone in a field
tied down just in case it changed its mind
about being earthbound.

it would be some understatement
to say I was not expecting it there
but not for a fraction of a second
did I mistake it for something else

so deeply ingrained is this
strange knowledge developed
quite without effort still fluent
in the arcane vocabulary
of those terrible and glory days.

Charming, jaunty, polite even, looking like a
little barn that wanted to fly
it is a machine which cannot hide its lineage:
spruce, Irish linen, cable and pulley
ingenuity; nor its purpose, Aldis sight,
Vickers and a panned up Lewis
on its Foster rail

a machine of destruction much cleverer
than it looks

but a kind of creature too, clearly wilful
with a fierce iron heart that needs a gentle touch
demanding to be understood and even
loved

or it will break
like a toy of a very large clumsy child
and break you too.

Seeing no-one around
I approached it tentatively
so as not to scare it away
it fluttered a little in the breeze as I neared
like a horse might shiver before
the bell

the obvious question spoken aloud, *Why are you here?*
Of course, no answer

it's clever but not that clever

but then, as I examined the almost
bathroom fittings that comprised
the cockpit workings, a clue
of a sort was provided by a distant
buzz and looking up some specks
on the horizon approaching quickly,
rather too quickly;

hand pump the fuel system, prime the engine,
select booster magneto, check wind, check
shutters, ...chocks away....

THE LAST BREAKFAST

Mr Watson ordered breakfast
this morning in French.
Oh no, there must be a mistake,
he doesn't speak French!
No, he spoke good French. I did
a Higher in it. We had a
good conversation before
the drugs took him away.

Christ, he kept that hidden!
true to his Edwardian upbringing
modest to the end never moaned
patiently waiting on the sun he
ay claimed would be along in time
broken at just 70 by all the
troubles of the century.
And now, we mounted final

guard around his bed while
we waited on him stepping
over to the other quarters.
Right at that last moment
before the bullet that didn't get you
finally got you I like to think
you were with your old mates
you told me off

in some estaminet ordering
eggs and chips in French
for the last time it was
always the last time for

some of them, young Lt Cowan
training to be the lawyer
he never became. *Tam, Don't...!*
you told him, and you'd no

sooner said it when he was
killed right there on the firestep.
It was a mad wicked thing,
but I never met finer people-
that's how life balances itself.
All those fine fellows who
got the wrong ticket home
just one now was waiting

to join their ranks perhaps
the finest of them all although
you would have strongly objected
to the compliment but knowing
something of life myself now
I stand by it
fraternal hard-working
kind considerate appreciative

of daily blessings uncomplaining
while the cancer bayoneted
you over and over
I was only a boy without
the words to shape my
understanding of the sheer immensity
of your decency
and so now Danny old soldier

Grandad, nearly fifty years

after your final roll call I salute
you and your kind and see
you with Jack and Pat easily
in my mind's eye loosening
your belt, taking off your
tammy and waiting to be
offered a seat.

*Excuse moi, Madame, pouvons nous avoir quelque chose
a manger?*

Blue Sky Thinking

AMERICAN GIRL

at 66 and 328.

Arched backwards making
a lovely curve that begs
your fingers to run over
smooth belly to the sky
just at that beautiful point before
she tips and falls down, down
like a stone into the void beneath
Oh, you so want to follow her there.

Turning heads of Tims and Tommies
those who thought their love
fixed forever on this or that
native beauty suddenly,
standing next to you, rendered
homely and plain their former
glamour now just common
reliability of any old she.

Sure, they love their old girl at home, but you know if they
could choose, where the tears would fall.

Too slow! Too stunned!
she gathers those who would gather others
tip to tip outstretched
sending them by storm suddenly
irresistibly delivered to their deserved
resting place and converting their
smoking carcases to little icons
neatly rowed beneath her window.

This ladies costume jewellery is also
her victory medals and the symbol
of the hard lesson taught
to the boasters shutting their mouths
forever with the strong
reminder that humiliation and ruin
is where beauty reveals her power.

BE COOL

the world a blur inside a box
inside a mighty roar
we as near to one as two
can ever be
now swooping still thrilling
as blue goes green
stomach about ear level
orange balls in front

black puffs behind
fingering that button
which is why I am here
everything I need to know
inside a little Norman arch
at eye level, no! not true,
everything I need to know
I already know

in front unexpectedly definitely
death personified as a machine
not some ugly crushing thing
but beautiful, simple in its
visible geometry as if designed
by an angel, maybe Lucifer.
I've never seen one before
but took it in my stride

and gave it a squirt to check
my medicine against its medicine
maybe I gave it a fright
certainly it shot off quickly

and then, things heating up,
so did I moving forward
and upwards into the cold
of the big blue sky.

In respect of the crossed lion, 602 sqn RAF.

PILOT'S NOTES FOR EXTREME RANGE MISSIONS WITH THE MITSUBISHI A6M (ZERO)

and the secret of life

lean to begin with, but still
strip down further
as if to its underpants
polish everything that sticks up or out
make it that bit slippier
take off the armour, remove the cannon
then remember
every single ounce has a cost in fuel
no matter how miniscule so,

take out everything you will not need for the day
scarf, tea flask, keepsakes, notebook, pencils,
pistol,
you won't be shooting anyone
and if it goes wrong
you need not worry
about the ending
for honour's sake.
Then go.

Undercarriage up as soon as you clear the deck
once the wheels are up
you're on life's home run
one way or another so,
fly looking at the rev counter, not airspeed
keep just that crucial fraction above stall

with the
leanest fuel mixture
that will spark.

**Let the wind do the work,
so work out in advance how you plan to use it.
Be aware of thermals and use them to gain height
which you trade for time as you glide down to
optimum altitude.**
Love the machine, really
listen to the engine
and give it your trust
to keep you out of the blue
it knows if you do or don't

make this your private religion
believe me, it knows
'wing and a prayer' is not
a cliché in this game.
I've got home on a sieve
empennage shot to ribbons
because I willed it
and that's the edge that will
see me win through

to touch down safely on deck
climb out the cockpit
and into your arms.

Bomber Command Tour

BOMBER COMMAND MONUMENT

There, 70 years on.

Pride of kinship
finally cleared of unjust infamy
swells to bursting
when I think of his role
in breaching that greatest of fortresses

built for the first thousand years
but reduced to a pile of cinders
and twisted steel in a thousand days.
He was twenty then.

Sitting in a metal box at 16,000 feet
not fully knowing I think that he
and his comrades were teaching
a lesson in hubris on a scale
previously reserved for gods.

I know he took no pleasure
in the making of that Landscape of Bones.
And thus, I believe, earned the reprieve
on the big scales of fate
that brought him home to family.

The four Brownings he sat behind
in his little office at the rear
might have helped a bit;
Tail-end Charlie, they called it
with British understatement.

If it sounds slightly humorous,
it wasn't.

Each trip tension like a whole life
lived in a night
waiting to be burst open
or torched, dishing out
the same on industrial scale,
block by city block.
They started it, we finished it.

He'd seen enough of death
in particularly spectacular forms
to be grateful for just getting out alive.
Why should he care for monuments?
Having built one in solid
blocks of courage minute by minute
in eight hour shifts.

But as life turns increasingly to memory
with the years the criticism
of those who would not have enjoyed
the same privilege under the eagle
must have hurt.
Which is why, I think, he unwittingly
built a monument of sorts in me
and from my boyish admiration
reflected back glory's shine
that was his by right.

A right put right too late
for him

but by the tightest of margins,
the wheels touching down
with the tanks reading empty,
just in time for the remaining old boys

to speak for those
who have made their final flight
through adversity to the stars.

The last line is the RAF's motto (Per Ardua ad Astra)
rendered in English.

BOMBER HARRIS

Formerly

famous for churches, medieval architecture,
brewing fine lager, served by fräuleins
imagined as racked and low cut
handmaidens of a religion soon
to face a time in the wilderness

all these were inconsequential;
utterly. When noting the major
manufacturing, crucial rail link,
various headquarters and army barracks,
and so, well due a visit

by the heavy team
after which he could note
with a neutrality which belied
and strangely confirmed his pride
shaded by smugness that it was

now none of them

its heart having been ripped out
the wound left un-cauterised
to fester well beyond the
primary blast zone and reach
into our own souls.

AN UNFORTUNATE SYNCHRONICITY

Load delivered and returning home
exhausts sparking more than usual
a beacon for every night fighter.
Most unsafe, skip decided
to take her down and
follow the roads on compass west
an unfortunate synchronicity

for some other early birds
on the same road.
The bomb aimer saw them
too late to fire and called
an excited warning to Benny

at the rear who wondered
for the briefest of moments,
as the big black bird rushed
over them at 100 feet and
laid the Brownings on them,
fire button already ready…
the four barrels pointing
like the finger of God,
whether this really was
the enemy seen in real form
at last and not a another
tragic accident which war
manufactures in quantities
like bullets.

The moment gone as he saw
the motorcycle
with machine gun sidecar
a little truck following, hardly escorting
a convent school breakfast club,
he saw the leather-coated figures look up
their mouths making the O
of the appropriate word

as they met their irresistible fate
on a Dutch road at 3.46am
of armour-piercing, tracer
and incendiary.
A sudden 400 rounds ripped
a sight not reducible to
any simile.
It was his job in the time
of fire and blood

landing with more than
the usual story of razing some city
known before from a geography lesson,
but all the time wondering,
over post-op breakfast
about the movement of that
vast mechanism whose perfect
timing of sequences that night
brought him to these men
as their executioner

and if and how that event
would somehow play forward
in time matching blood for blood

the unfortunate synchronicity switched
to line him up with his executioner
who was already eating breakfast
unwittingly in preparation.

THE CURE

a one-man carousel
operated by you
kid's dream come true
spin as much as you like
there's always a catch
with fun
it'll kill you

and you can kill with it
so that squares that

you couldn't make this up
a view with drama in Technicolour
not beautiful, too big for that
awesome the vastness
a brightness
I understand what it's like
to be an atom

this mad thing I'm in
lovely orange, killing black

so fast it seemed the sky
had stopped except it
everybody's having a go
swopping medicine; my turn:
Holy Christ,... he's coming for me!
a loooooooong squirt
counting in twenties times four
80-160-240-320-400-480-560......

at this moment time is not time
and I am not me

reassuring in its wonderful
clattering madness, my machine
before it melts something will
prevail here soon, then
a line of silver dollars
danced along the wing's curve
and as quickly turned to little flames

and then Whoosh, it's gone
more a bomb than a bomb

after this I will sit
in my garden, smoke,
talk football, watch my children grow
and become old gently
and not feel the least
bit self-conscious about
any day the future brings.

LIVING YOUR ART

Wagner; creating that place
a lebensraum where truth and love combine
and consequences are to be endured
where loyalty is the greatest of virtues.
Because it is.

Identifying that place on the big map
where the consequences of all the thinking
will be endured
and where loyalty will prove itself
the greatest of virtues.
Because it is.

Tuning up their instruments
in the pit for the big show
annotating the sheets with pencil memos
leaving nothing to chance
demanding to bring the house down
for *his* sake.

Loading her up
in the pit for the big show
synchronising the Brownings
feeding it night tracer, incendiary, AP,
again and again in specific order
leaving nothing to chance
or the Luftwaffe.

Conductor taps his baton
bringing odd hoots and screechings
to a sudden halt

as
Skip, on a nod from the flight engineer,
pulls back the throttles
and the Merlins' measured rhythmic thump
races to a might roar that vibrates the bones
and airborne dust alike.

Tannhauser; the swooping overture opens
as the Dutch coast is crossed
and German air defences begin their own
overture.
The nachtjadgers playing the role of Valkyries.
Actually, they really are!

Point, counterpoint;
the utterly unmusical single note of the Merlins
matched by the beautiful choirs and strings
leading deeper and deeper
into the manically overwrought
worlds which must collide as absolutes
meet in mutual destruction.

Meanwhile, at 18,000 feet
400 Lancasters carry their own
version of Gotterdammerung
to the concert.

The conductor waves the baton.
Freudig begrüßen wir die edle halle,
wo kunst und frieden immer nur verweil,
wo lange noch der frohe ruf erschalle:
Thüringens fürsten, Landgraf Hermann, Heil!

And the bomb aimer sights up
in English, a prosaic reply;
Steady, steady, ok, I'll take it now, Skip.
Okay, okay, okay, nearly, nearly there...
.........right,.. okay, ehhh...bombs gone,
.. on the button. Let's go home...

That wonderful passionate chorus leading
your soul to wing to Heaven (or Valhalla)
as eight 1000lb bombs (with incendiaries)
leave their bay to join the finale
in Hell

and then, the crescendo;
Landgraf Hermann, Heil!
to bring down the house
as imagined by Wagner

writing music with an apocalyptic edge
for a future he would not see
whose sweep and grandeur places
you in a world of extremes
grand passions, iron resolve, mysterious pacts
that demand silent obedience.

Lovers broken by fate.
And, in the hysteria and collapse
of their world, the true German finds comfort
in their loyalty.

As the British settle down
(the lucky ones, that is)
for a well-earned fry up
and a cup of tea.

Enemies

DAS REICH

We few, we happy few,
we band of brothers...

(foxhole, MG42, Falaise gap)

Looking along that metre
of death as it played
its single killing note
without pleasure to some
distant figures who just fell over
without the least drama
well,...as viewed from
the friendlier end of trouble.

If you dish this fare out
in such generous proportions
you must expect to get it back
and in that exchange you will
not see this day through to its end
as a door slammed shut,
violently suddenly.

Don't grudge the loss
who knows what misery
life might have contained
if you lived to carry this day
to a scorched future
don't grudge those who flee
your gift to them
their lives as nothings

pain and pride the currency
of hardness the price of loyalty
your truth the truth
a lepers mark to a future afraid;
afraid of you, afraid of their guilt,
afraid of *it* contained within
the ring the promise that will
be fulfilled at the fulfilling time
when they come back as heroes.

It always ends like this
all through history regardless
of the rights and wrongs of the cause
the drones escape to carry on while
the cream is wiped off the top
and then denied.

ALSO AVAILABLE

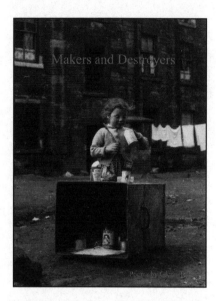

Makers and Destroyers

Glasgow; what's gone? The author examines the hammers and tongs, coal-fired world that was replaced and improved by what's came.

Or maybe not. We need a judge and jury on this; I bagsy the judge, yous can be the jury.

The Belt Room

A cross-my-heart true collection about some more-than-average tough schools during the '60s. It especially considers the use of corporal punishment (the belt) as a standard pedagogic technique; the author is well qualified to comment.